FRED VAN LENTE ★ RYAN DUNLAVEY

ACTION PRESIDENTS

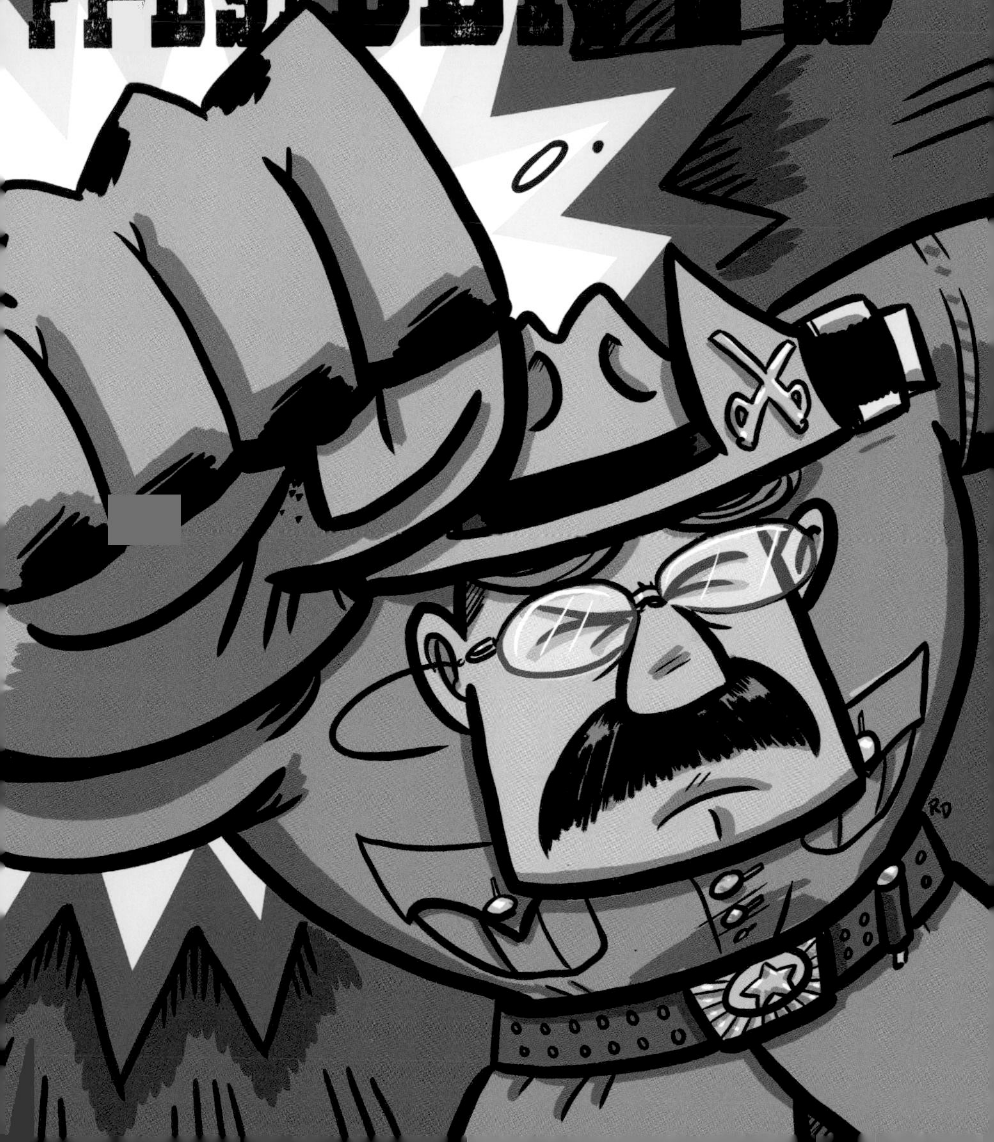

#3

FRED VAN LENTE ★ RYAN DUNLAVEY

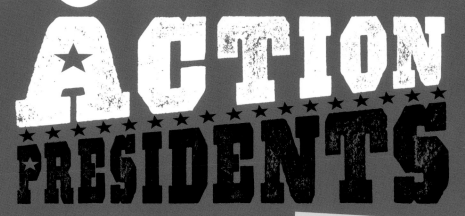

ACTION PRESIDENTS

REAL HISTORY!
FAKE JOKES!

THEODORE ROOSEVELT!

HARPER
alley

An Imprint of HarperCollinsPublishers

Harper Alley is an imprint of HarperCollins Publishers.

Action Presidents #3: Theodore Roosevelt!
Copyright © 2020 by Ryan Dunlavey and Fred Van Lente
Color assistant and colorist pp 21-25, 72-83 and 86-99: Aaron Polk
All rights reserved. Manufactured in Slovenia.
No part of this book may be used or reproduced in any manner whatsoever without written
permission except in the case of brief quotations embodied in critical articles and reviews. For
information address HarperCollins Children's Books, a division of HarperCollins Publishers,
195 Broadway, New York, NY 10007.
www.harpercollinschildrens.com

Library of Congress Control Number: 2018941362
ISBN 978-0-06-289124-2 (trade bdg.)
ISBN 978-0-06-289123-5 (pbk.)

The artist used Adobe Photoshop and Adobe Illustrator
to create the digital illustrations for this book.
20 21 22 23 24   GPS   10 9 8 7 6 5 4 3 2 1

First Edition

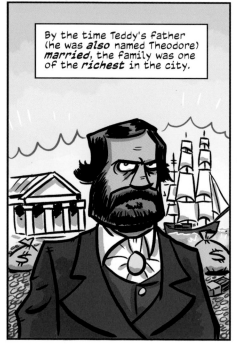

The *Civil War* divided the Roosevelt household. Martha refused to let Teddy Senior join the Union Army, where he might fight against her relatives.

In those days, if you got drafted into the army, you could *pay* $300 for someone to go fight instead of you – a sum most people couldn't afford.

Teddy Senior *could*, so he did just that.

Still, Dad wanted to help, so President Lincoln sent him to Union camps, where he used his banking knowledge to tell the troops to *save* their pay for their families instead of *wasting* it.

Meanwhile, Mom – with the help of *Teedie* (Teddy Junior's childhood nickname) – assembled "care packages" for Confederate troops to be smuggled through Union blockades.

Teedie knew his mother loved the Confederacy, so when she punished him, he prayed hard for Union victories.

DEAR LORD, PLEASE MAKE SURE *"HONEST"* ABE AND THE BLUE-COATS KICK THE REBELS' BUTTS!

!!!

THAT'LL SHOW MAMA! AMEN!

Few thought Teedie would *live* long enough to see the war's *end*, though.

He was a small, sickly child, suffering from a number of ailments such as *asthma*, a disease that makes breathing difficult.

Teedie's parents did everything they could to help him. One of his earliest memories was of his father walking him around his room until he could breathe again.

WHEEEEEEZE....!

Dad would take him on extra-fast carriage rides to force air into his lungs.

"THEODORE, YOU HAVE THE *MIND* BUT YOU HAVE NOT THE *BODY*, AND WITHOUT THE *HELP* OF THE BODY, THE MIND CANNOT GO AS FAR AS IT SHOULD.

"YOU MUST *MAKE* YOUR BODY. IT IS HARD *DRUDGERY* TO MAKE ONE'S BODY, BUT I KNOW YOU WILL DO IT."

OKAY, FATHER –

– I WILL *MAKE* MY BODY!

Teedie *exercised* every day with weights and horizontal bars.

Progress came slowly. He was always short, and his bad eyesight made him wear thick glasses, so he was often picked on by bullies.

"The worst feature," Teedie wrote, "was that when I finally tried to *fight* them I discovered that either one *singly* could not only handle me with *easy contempt...*"

"...but handle me so as not to hurt me much and yet to prevent *my* doing *any* damage whatever in *return.*"

Teedie's dad allowed him to learn *boxing* to defend himself.

He was fascinated by *sports* of all kinds – fighting, hunting, fishing, hiking, riding – you name it.

9

One day, Teedie's mom sent him up Broadway to get *strawberries* for breakfast from the market.

A dead seal was laid out on a slab in the market when he arrived.

Teedie loved stories of the sea, and the sight of this animal fascinated him.

CLANG!

He couldn't stop staring at it, and wondered what adventures it had while it was alive.

He even got his hands on the seal's skull and brought it home with him!

THAT'S NOT STRAWBERRIES!

From then on, animals fascinated Teedie and he filled his home with them:

The Roosevelt Museum

HELLO, HELLO, WELCOME TO OUR GRAND *REOPENING*, ONE AND ALL! *DEEEE-LIGHTED* YOU COULD MAKE IT!

THIS IS OUR NEW LOCATION IN THE *UPSTAIRS BACK HALL*, AS MOTHER MADE ME MOVE MY TAXIDERMY PROJECTS OUT OF MY *ROOM*.

SOME OF THE MAIDS, YOU SEE, *OBJECTED*.

"EEEK!"

PLEASE, *PLEASE,* NO PUSHING OR LINE-CUTTING! EVERYONE WILL HAVE A TURN...

...TO GAPE AT THE *MARVELS* COLLECTED FROM THE ROOSEVELT FAMILY'S TRAVELS 'ROUND THE *WORLD*!

YOUR SHOCKED SILENCE SPEAKS *VOLUMES.*

UM, YEAH...

IT'S... *NICE?*

ActionEarth

OF COURSE IT'S NICE! *MUSEOLOGY* IS IN MY BLOOD.

MY FATHER HELPED FOUND THE *AMERICAN MUSEUM OF NATURAL HISTORY* ON CENTRAL PARK WEST, DON'T YOU KNOW....

When he was old enough to go to college, Teed—er—Teddy (a nickname he hated) got into famed *Harvard University.*

He hoped to become a **scientist** but was disappointed to find Harvard didn't let their natural history students leave the **laboratory**.

>SIGH<

Also, he started dating a woman, **Alice Lee**, who thought his interest in taxidermy was...well, pretty **gross**.

EEEEEEEE!

So he gave up on **science**, though he wasn't sure what he wanted to do with his life *instead*.

Meanwhile, his father was trying to continue in government service. President Rutherford B. Hayes asked Teddy Senior to be the Collector of Customs for the Port of New York.

Prez #19
(1877-1881)

In the 19th century, before many of the taxes we have today were passed, fees on goods coming into the USA from other countries, or "customs," were one of the main ways the government earned money so it could operate.

Because New York City had the biggest seaport in the country, a lot of money passed in and out of its customhouse. That meant there was a lot of temptation for whoever was Collector of Customs to steal some of that money.

14

THE SPOILS SYSTEM...

...was the 19th-century term for how government jobs were handed out in those days. When Andrew Jackson won the election of 1828, Senator William L. Marcy declared:

"TO THE VICTOR BELONG THE SPOILS!"

("Spoils," meaning the *loot* a winning army plunders from a defeated city!)

Prez #7 (1829-1837)

For decades afterward, whenever *one* party came into power, it kicked all of the people belonging to the *losing* party out of their jobs in the government, or *"Civil Service."*

WAAAAAAAAAAA!

This led to a lot of chaos, confusion, and inefficiency in providing services.

Even more important, the Spoils System was a great way for political parties to *bribe* people for influence and votes...

...offering to provide voters with *cushy jobs* in exchange for their support.

President Hayes named honest, already-rich Teddy Senior as Collector of Customs to *fight* this kind of corruption.

But lots of politicians really, really *liked* the Spoils System and so they decided to make an *example* of Teddy Senior.

His appointment had to be approved by the United States Senate.

At first, pro-Spoiler senators just delayed and delayed and *delayed* taking up Teddy Senior's nomination.

DAYS TO HEARING: 2

DAYS TO HEARING: 26

Teddy Senior was wracked with horrible *chest pains* during the process.

When Spoilers finally succeeded in rejecting his nomination 31 to 25, he *collapsed*.

It turned out he had developed a tumor in his bowels, and he *died* on February 9, 1878 — only a few months after his first exposure to *politics*.

DAYS TO HEARING: 65

DAYS TO HEARING: 0

Teddy received a big inheritance from his father, but he was still no closer to knowing what he wanted to do with his life.

He had been studying *law* in college but didn't like that lawyers had to argue on behalf of their *clients*, not on behalf of what was *right*.

He busied himself by working on a book called *The Naval War of 1812*, about the sea battles the US Navy fought with Britain after the Revolution.

Teddy argued that a mighty *fleet* was necessary to maintain America's strength in the world.

Strangely enough, Teddy was *drawn* to the dark world that *killed* his father.

Teddy found himself hanging out at *Morton Hall*, the New York City headquarters of the *Republicans*, his father's and President Lincoln's party.

It was a seedy place full of back-room dealmakers.

He *loved* it.

WAIT — WHY IS THE **REPUBLICAN** HALL FILLED WITH **ELEPHANTS?**

THE TWO MAJOR PARTIES IN THE USA HAVE HAD **ANIMAL MASCOTS** FOR A LONG TIME!

WHEN **ANDREW JACKSON** WAS RUNNING FOR PRESIDENT IN 1828, HIS ENEMIES SAID HE WAS AS **STUBBORN** AS A **DONKEY!**

PROVING HIS FOES **RIGHT**, JACKSON EMBRACED THE LABEL AND SOON **ALL** HIS DEMOCRATS WERE KNOWN AS DONKEYS!

Tammany Hall (NYC Democratic HQ)

REPUBLICAN POLITICAL CARTOONIST **THOMAS NAST** WAS ANNOYED WITH HIS PARTY IN 1874, AND DEPICTED THEM AS A BIG, SLOW **ELEPHANT** COMPARED TO THE DEMOCRATIC DONKEY.

Thomas Nast (1840-1902), "Father of the American Cartoon"

18

Teddy's family, *horrified*, said Teddy Senior would have **hated** it if Junior went into politics, because it was filled with *"rough and brutal and unpleasant"* men.

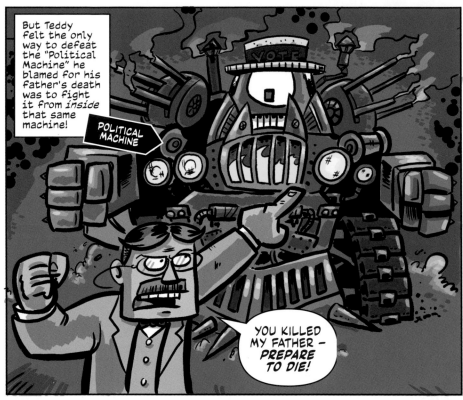

But Teddy felt the only way to defeat the "Political Machine" he blamed for his father's death was to fight it from *inside* that same machine!

POLITICAL MACHINE

VOTE

YOU KILLED MY FATHER — *PREPARE TO DIE!*

NYC REPUBLICANS SAW THE ADVANTAGE OF HAVING AN *OLD-MONEY* MAN LIKE TEDDY ON THEIR SIDE AND GOT HIM ELECTED TO THE *NEW YORK STATE LEGISLATURE* IN 1881.

BUT WHAT ABOUT *SANTA?*

ENOUGH ABOUT SANTA!

THIS ISN'T "ACTION SANTA!"

"My first days in the Legislature were much like those of a boy in a *strange school*," Teddy wrote.

"My fellow legislators and I eyed one another with mutual *distrust*."

"Each of us chose his *seat*..."

"...and then, in a week or two, we began to drift into *groups* according to our several *affinities* (similarities)."

He also had to contend with *bullies*. When an assemblyman made fun of his jacket...

"WON'T MAMA'S BOY *CATCH COLD?*"

...Teddy punched him down — *three times!*

"DO NOT HIT AT *ALL* IF IT CAN BE AVOIDED...

"...BUT *NEVER* HIT SOFTLY!"

When another assemblyman, ex-prize fighter "Big John" MacManus, said he planned to grab him and toss him up in a blanket, Teddy warned him:

HA HA HA HA @#!

"I'LL *KICK* YOU! I'LL *BITE* YOU!"

Big John got the message.

Teddy swore to defeat government *corruption* in New York State, just as his father tried to do in the customhouse.

Once, crooked legislators held up an *honest* railway law from being passed.

Teddy knew some of the assemblymen opposing the bill were "pretty *rough* characters."

He wrote:

"There was a broken chair in the room..."

"...and I got a leg of it loose and put it down beside me where it was not visible, but where I might get at it in a hurry if necessary."

Teddy announced he was going to introduce the bill anyway, and a riot almost broke out among the opponents...

...but then Teddy produced the chair leg.

WAP!

He didn't *use* it. He just put it by his side on the desk...

TUNK!

...and his enemies left him alone.

SIT!

Thus proving one of Teddy's favorite and most famous sayings, which he said was a West African proverb:

"SPEAK SOFTLY AND CARRY A BIG STICK...

"...YOU WILL GO FAR."

Then, the day one of Teddy's most important *reform* bills was put to a vote, *tragedy* struck.

His wife, *Alice*, back at home in his mother's New York mansion, was about to give birth to their first child. In the state capital, Albany, Teddy received a telegram that said:

Congratulations! Alice gave birth to a healthy girl last night, though she is now only fairly well.

WELL DONE, OLD BOY!

But then *another* telegram arrived:

Alice has taken a turn for the worse. Come immediately.

!!!

He rushed home to Manhattan as fast as he could.

FASTER! *FASTER!!*

When he got to the Roosevelt mansion on 57th Street, he made a terrible discovery:

On the top floor, his wife was dying of *kidney disease.*

On another floor, his mother had *typhoid fever.*

Mother Roosevelt died at three a.m. that morning... Alice at two p.m. that same day.

Teddy was heartbroken. He left his newborn baby girl, named Alice after her mother, in the care of his sister.

Both his mother and wife had passed on February 14...*Valentine's Day.*

He rarely spoke of Alice again.

And he vanished from Manhattan...from New York State politics...

The US Army had driven Native Americans off these lands years before, and it had been taken over by rough-and-tumble *settlers*.

But Teddy earned the respect of cowboys by *being* a cowboy, helping rustle up cows and herd them to market.

I SAY, *CEASE* YOUR *FORWARD MOMENTUM* THERE, MY FINE "*DOGGIE*"!

WE, UH, USUALLY JUST SAY "*WHOA.*"

These frontiersmen were just as suspicious of him as the assemblymen in Albany had been.

He was amazed by the various kinds of people he found. He loved the nicknames:

Dutchy

Buckskin

Texas Jack

Red Jim

Kentuck

Bronco Bill

Bear Jones

Frenchy

Plainsmen, he said, "all have a certain curious *similarity* to each other; existence in the West seems to put the same *stamp* upon each and every one of them."

He knew a bunch of Bill Joneses: *Three Seven* Bill Jones, *Texas* Bill Jones, even *Hell-Roaring* Bill Jones.

I'M THE SHERIFF! *YEE-HAW!*

Some Westerners got their nicknames because of the **things** they did.

WHY ARE YOU NAMED "LIVER-EATING" JOHNSON?

'CAUSE **ONCE** I ATE A GUY'S **LIVER!**

ALL RIGHT... GOOD TO KNOW....

One false move could brand a cowboy forever: one guide he employed was named "Muddy Bill" because a horse once threw him into a big mud puddle.

AND THEY **NEVER** LET ME **FORGET** IT!

Likewise, Teddy's cowboys teased him with the nickname "Old Hasten Forward Quickly There"...

I SAY! HASTEN FORWARD **QUICKLY** THERE, FELLOWS!

...the fancy phrase he once used to tell them to **hurry.**

But when Teddy first met **new** cowboys, the first thing they couldn't resist making fun of were his **spectacles.**

GASP! HIS EYES ARE MADE OF **GLASS!** HE'S SOME KINDA **MACHINE-MAN!**

One cold night he was riding the range looking for lost horses when he stopped for the night at a saloon.

TAKE *THAT*, CLOCK, FOR *TICKIN'* BEHIND MY *BACK!* HAW!

He wrote: "Inside the room were several men, who, including the bartender, were wearing the kind of smile worn by men who are making believe to *like* what they *don't like.*"

HEY, GET A LOAD OF *FOUREYES!*

GUESS WHAT, EVERYBODY! *FOUREYES* IS GONNA TREAT US ALL TO A DRINK!

HA, HA, VERY FUNNY.

30

"When he went down he struck the corner of the bar with his head."

KRAK

GOOD WORK, FOUREY—UH, **STRANGER!**

HE WAS A WILD AND SCARY DRUNK!

"When my assailant came to, he went down to the station and left on a freight (a train carrying cargo)."

MAIL

Soon Teddy had earned the respect of his employees and neighbors to the point where Hell-Roaring Bill Jones made Teddy a deputy sheriff.

BULLY!

"Wonderful!" (in those days)

SHERIFF

Teddy's tin star came in handy when he woke up one morning to discover his riverboat had been stolen.

He soon realized the culprits were a notorious gang of horse thieves led by long-haired "Redhead" Finnegan.

MWAHAHAHAH!!

Teddy had his men build *another* boat while he worked on the latest book he was writing (yes, *really*).

He knew he'd have time to catch the thieves because a big blizzard moved in, slowing their escape.

Teddy and his two ranch hands took off after Redhead's gang.

HASTEN FORWARD *QUICKLY* THERE!

They drifted along through massive ice walls surrounding them on both sides of the river. Sometimes the ice would break off and crash into the water with a terrifying sound.

YAAAH! WHAT WAS THAT?!

CHOOOM

They found abandoned tepees, shot a few deer for breakfast, but saw no one.

Finally, later in the afternoon of April 1 (*April Fool's!*) they stumbled across the stolen craft.

THERE!

34

Somehow, in the midst of all his other adventures, Teddy found time to go hunting elk and bear in the nearby mountains.

Even though he liked shooting animals, he made a distinction between *"fair play"* hunting and what he thought of as *"butchery."*

He saw hunting as something of a game – a *deadly* game but a *game* all the same – between his prey and him.

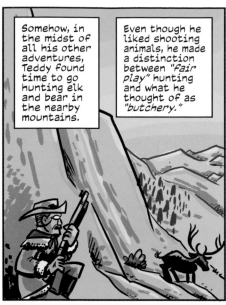

Unfair tricks such as hiding for deer behind a camouflaged blind were against the *"rules."*

LOOK OUT!

He was horrified by the mass killing of the *buffalo* by meat and fur hunters that had made the great mammals all but *extinct.*

With each trip out to the wilderness he came back to find a little more of the frontier taken over by *civilization.*

WHERE'D ALL *THIS* COME FROM?!

IT LOOKS LIKE A REAL *TOWN* NOW!

More and more settlers moved into the once "pure" wilderness, troubling Teddy.

THERE GOES THE NEIGHBORHOOD!

U-SETTLE

"ONE OF THE CHIEF ATTRACTIONS OF THE LIFE OF THE WILDERNESS IS ITS RUGGED AND STALWART *DEMOCRACY*; THERE EVERY MAN STANDS FOR WHAT HE ACTUALLY *IS*, AND CAN SHOW HIMSELF TO *BE*."

Teddy worried that the more *wilderness* America lost, the more it lost that *natural democracy* so important to her national character.

The land wasn't managed at all. People brought too many cows to graze and soon there was no grass left for any of them.

In 1886, Teddy decided it was time at last to return to New York City.

Teddy had been making visits back East this whole time and had struck up a romance with a childhood sweetheart, *Edith Carow*, and they planned to *marry.*

What was left of his cattle herd would be wiped out by the historically *awful* winter.

Some cows were so dumb it didn't occur to them to face *away* from the snow, so it filled their mouths, *choking* them!

Thousands more were buried in massive *snowdrifts.*

His old friends in the NYC Republican Party nominated him to become the city's mayor, but he lost.

Teddy married Edith and started a new family on his Long Island estate, *Sagamore Hill.*

See "Places to Visit" at the back of the book.

Teddy wrote books about his ranching adventures. What he earned from his *pen* became his main source of income.

He also wrote about history a lot. Two of his most popular books were *The Winning of the West* and *The History of the City of New York.*

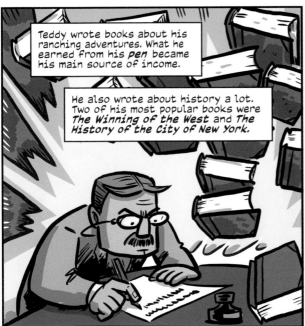

HISTORY IS —

— JUST BULLY!

AW, YEAH!

SLAP!

Teddy didn't take criticism well. When George *Bird* Grinnell, editor of *Forest and Stream* magazine and founder of the Audubon Society, wrote a bad review of his book *Hunting Trips of a Ranchman*, Teddy burst into his office!

HOW *DARE* YOU, SIR?!

"SQUARK?!"

not actual bird

But once they got to talking, they discovered they had too much in common to *not* be fast friends!

Together they founded the first *"conservationist"* organization in America, the *Boone and Crockett Club*, named after two of the most famous frontiersmen in American history...

...dedicated not just to the *exploration* of the great wildernesses of the United States, but their *preservation* for future generations.

Davy Crockett (1786-1836)

Daniel Boone (1734-1820)

Still, Teddy was finding it difficult to make ends meet, and he was itching to return to *politics* and to fight for his pet causes.

WOOF

MEOW!

Pet Cause

The new Republican president, *Benjamin Harrison*, asked if he would like to be *Civil Service Commissioner*, the person in charge of the agency that handed out federal government jobs.

Prez #23 (1889-1893)

THE COMMISH

Everyone in the capital was sick of talking about Civil Service Reform...but Teddy never got sick of talking about *anything.*

UGH! THIS AGAIN...!

SO BORRRRRING...!

REFORM! REFORM! REFORM!

He fought for a *written exam* to see whether or not people who applied for government jobs were *qualified* for them.

TOSS!

SEE, YOU'RE NOT THE ONLY ONE WHO HATES *TESTS.*

THERE OUGHTA BE A *LAW* AGAINST 'EM!!

YOINK!

Teddy argued that *testing* people for jobs was the only way to make sure that *everyone* had the same opportunity, regardless of who they *knew,* or who their *parents* were, or what *party* they belonged to.

NO TEST, NO JOB!

BOOOOOO!

In other words, Teddy thought of the American Civil Service Exam the same way he did about the American wilderness: it was all about *democracy.*

Commissioner Teddy was disgusted by the corruption of white officials on Native American reservations and the terrible conditions in which many of their residents lived.

He tried to get the exam extended to the Indian Bureau, but the president blocked him.

BLOCKED AGAIN... BY "THE *LITTLE GREY MAN* IN THE WHITE HOUSE."

PRRRRRRR

Teddy grew to hate Harrison, even though they were both *Republicans.*

Teddy discovered that the post offices in Baltimore, Maryland, were especially corrupt, full of unqualified people who got jobs just because they were *Republicans.*

"NAME *FIVE* NEW ENGLAND STATES!"

"ENGLAND, IRELAND, SCOTLAND, WALES, AND CORK!"

THAT'S *OLD* ENGLAND, YOU KNOW-NOTHING!

BUT MY UNCLE *JUMBO* SAYS I'M DOING A *GREAT* JOB!!

Teddy and the Postmaster General's *epic battles* over corruption were big news and badly embarrassed the Harrison administration.

The Republican press attacked Teddy for *betraying* his own party.

It was a tough few years, but on the days he found himself walking past the White House:

"MY HEART WOULD BEAT A LITTLE FASTER AS THE THOUGHT CAME TO ME THAT POSSIBLY – *POSSIBLY* – I WOULD SOME DAY OCCUPY IT *AS* PRESIDENT."

WAIT, WAIT, WAIT. I'M *CONFUSED.*

I THOUGHT PRESIDENT HARRISON *HIRED* TEDDY TO DO *JUST* WHAT HE WAS DOING! SO WHY'D EVERYBODY GET SO *MAD?*

RIGHT, THE PROBLEM IS...

...most people **want** to **look** like they're doing the right thing...

I NEED YOU TO QUOTE-UNQUOTE "FIGHT CORRUPTION," NUDGE, NUDGE, WINK, WINK...

...but they don't want the **trouble** caused by actually **doing** the right thing!

"MY DUTY WAS STAND **WITH** EVERYONE WHILE HE WAS **RIGHT**..."

"...AND TO STAND **AGAINST** HIM WHEN HE WAS **WRONG**!"

SNAP!

BUT I THOUGHT WE WERE FRIENDS!!

Ironically, the corruption in the Harrison administration that Teddy helped to root out contributed to the president's defeat to a former Democratic president, *Grover Cleveland*.

SIGH...

HEE HAW!

COMMISH

Prez #22 *and* 24 (1885-1889 and 1893-1897)

As soon as the second *Cleveland* administration came into power in Washington, the Republican Teddy was *replaced* as Civil Service Commissioner by a Democrat...per the *Spoils System!*

This set the main **pattern** for Teddy's career in government.

He'd get **hired** to do a job – he'd make people **mad** when he did the job – he'd get **fired** –

– then he'd get **hired again** by someone else who **said** they cared about **reform.**

Case in point:

When Teddy returned to **New York City** in 1895, the mayor made him president of the **Police Commission.**

The NYPD was mired in corruption and inefficiency. It was commonplace for crooks to pay **bribes** to cops for them to look the other way.

I'M GONNA CLEAN UP THIS TOWN!

WHAM!

N.Y.P.D.

The Chief of Police himself was worth as much as **$350,000** thanks in part to various kickback and bribery schemes.

Until, *once again,* his political enemies gave him the boot.

HOW *DARE* YOU DO *EXACTLY* WHAT I *ASKED* YOU TO!

YOU'D THINK I'D GET *USED* TO THIS BY NOW....

N.Y.P.D

POLICE

TEDDY! COME BACK TO *WASHINGTON!* THERE'S A NEW *REPUBLICAN* PRESIDENT, WILLIAM MCKINLEY!

U.S. NAVY

Teddy's Republican friends asked him to be Assistant Secretary of the Navy.

LET ME GUESS — THERE USED TO BE A *DEMOCRAT* SITTING HERE!

Teddy wanted the job pretty bad.

YOU... WANT...TO BE...IN THE NAVY...!

YES...THE *NAVY*...!

As the author of *The Naval War of 1812,* he was already a respected authority on sea warfare.

Still, President McKinley wasn't convinced.

"GIVE HIM A **CHANCE** TO PROVE THAT HE **CAN** BE PEACEFUL."

"I WANT **PEACE**, AND I AM TOLD THAT YOUR FRIEND THEODORE — WHOM I KNOW ONLY **SLIGHTLY** — IS ALWAYS GETTING INTO **ROWS** (FIGHTS) WITH EVERYBODY."

Prez #25 (1897-1901)

RAAAAH!

President McKinley's fears soon came true.

MORE! MORE! MORE!

Teddy thought the navy didn't have enough **ships** and demanded a massive military buildup.

McKinley had served in the Union Army at **Antietam**, one of the bloodiest battles of the Civil War. He knew battlefield horrors **firsthand**.

Pop! Pop!

WAR! WAR! WAR!

To the president, Teddy, who had **never** served in the military, had no idea what he was talking about and so he ignored him.

49

Teddy wanted more ships largely because of the scary situation in *Cuba*, only **90 miles** from Florida.

The island had been part of the **Spanish empire** since 1492, when Christopher Columbus first **sailed the ocean blue.**

I'VE GOT A **BAD** FEELING ABOUT THIS.

YOU NEVER WANT TO TRY NEW THINGS!

Native Cubans

By the time Teddy joined the navy, Cuban rebels fighting for *independence* controlled much of Cuba's jungles and farms while the Spanish Army controlled the cities.

The Spanish governor tried to **weaken** the rebellion by herding much of the rural population into **concentration camps.**

More than 400,000 Cubans died from starvation and disease in the camps, horrifying the world.

American public opinion grew more and more strongly anti-Spanish.

50

THE MONROE DOCTRINE...

...had been a cornerstone of American foreign policy since the presidency of *James Monroe* in 1823.

HEY! CUT IT OUT, GRABBY!

He said that the United States would consider any European power trying to take over a country in North, South, or Central America to be an *enemy* of the USA.

USA

Prez #5 (1817-1825)

SLAP!

SOUTH AMERICA

Teddy tried to use the Monroe Doctrine to justify helping Cuba's rebels, but it didn't apply because Cuba was an *old* colony.

LEMME AT 'EM, LEMME AT 'EM!!

Still, President McKinley bowed to public pressure and sent a single warship, the *Maine*, to Havana, Cuba's capital, to "*look after American interests.*"

Translation:

"HEY, SPAIN...WE'RE *WATCHING YOU!* BEHAVE!"

The ship's forecastle was filled with *gunpowder* and surrounded by *wiring.* Any short circuit or related *electrical* problem could have provided the *spark* to ignite the explosion.

Many others, including Teddy, called it an *attack.* Some said that Spain floated a *mine* at the ship to get the Americans out of their hair.

TERRIBLE, *TERRIBLE* NEWS ABOUT THE *MAINE,* ROOSEVELT!

INDEED IT IS, SIR!

Navy Sec'y John D. Long (*Teddy's Boss*)

IT LOOKS *BAD* FOR SPAIN, BUT A THOROUGH *INVESTIGATION* WILL HAVE TO BE MADE OF THE DISASTER BEFORE WE MAKE ANY *HASTY DECISIONS*, NO?

WELL, I AM GOING TO TAKE THE REST OF THE DAY OFF — I HAVE BEEN HAVING A LOT OF ACHES AND PAINS, AND THIS *ELECTRICAL MASSAGE MACHINE* IS QUITE HELPFUL!

(100% true)

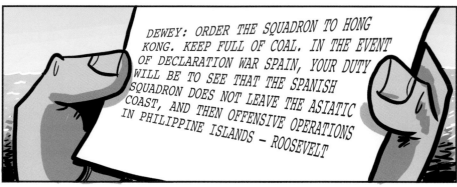

DEWEY: ORDER THE SQUADRON TO HONG KONG. KEEP FULL OF COAL. IN THE EVENT OF DECLARATION WAR SPAIN, YOUR DUTY WILL BE TO SEE THAT THE SPANISH SQUADRON DOES NOT LEAVE THE ASIATIC COAST, AND THEN OFFENSIVE OPERATIONS IN PHILIPPINE ISLANDS — ROOSEVELT

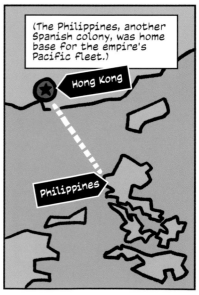

(The Philippines, another Spanish colony, was home base for the empire's Pacific fleet.)

Hong Kong

Philippines

Though there was no evidence *who* had bombed the *Maine*,
if it *had* been bombed, the incident *ruined*
relations between Spain and the US.

Congress passed a resolution demanding Spain *leave* Cuba, so Spain broke off diplomatic relations with the US.

When the US Navy *blockaded* Cuba on April 21, Spain declared war on the US on April 24.

Congress declared war on Spain on April 25...

I DID IT FIRST! ME!

NO! ME!

...*backdating* the declaration for April 21, so America could say *they* technically declared war *first*.

I *QUIT*, SIR!

WHAT — *WHY*, ROOSEVELT? A *WAR* IS STARTING — ISN'T THAT WHAT YOU ALWAYS *WANTED*?

INDEED!

SO NOW I'M GOING TO GO *FIGHT* IN IT!

?!

Meanwhile, an ocean away, Teddy's early war preparations *paid off.*

Commodore Dewey's ships sailed to the Philippines and caught the Spanish Fleet by complete surprise on May 1, 1898, sinking *all* of it!

The United States had seized the main Spanish possession in the *Pacific*, and was now moving on Cuba, its biggest colony in the *Atlantic.*

The United States Army deployed from Tampa, Florida, was the largest armed force ever to leave American shores (up until that point).

Roosevelt was *stunned* to learn that not only was there no room on the transport ships for all of his *men*, there was absolutely no room for any but a *few* horses.

NOT DEE-LIGHTED!

HAW! WE'RE NOT TEDDY'S ROUGH *RIDERS* — BUT *"WOOD'S WEARY WALKERS"!*

The Americans couldn't get close enough to unload what few horses they did bring, so they were simply dumped in the ocean and expected to swim their way to the beach.

SHOVE!

WHINNY

SPLASH!

The panicked animals started swimming out to sea!

But a bugler on shore blew a cavalry call...

BUDPUD DABUPBUP A BUD-DABUP BA-BUP

...which turned them around and brought them to shore.

WHEW!

To get across the mountains to Cuba's cities, the "Rough Walkers" had to march through a pass the locals called *Las Guásimas*, after its *hog-nut trees* (*guácimas*).

The commander of cavalry, Major General Joseph ("Fighting Joe") Wheeler, was an old *Confederate Army* veteran who sometimes forgot which *war* he was in.

THIS WAY, BOYS, TO WASHINGTON, DC! WE'LL *WHIP* THE UNION AND THROW LYIN' ABE LINCOLN IN CUFFS YET!

NO, NO, NO... THIS ISN'T THE CIVIL...

June 24, 1898

WAIT! LOOK!

BODY'S STILL WARM! THE *YANKEES* MUST BE NEAR!

ROOSEVELT, YOU LEAD THE ROUGH RIDERS THAT WAY, THROUGH THE WOODS, WHILE THE REST OF US CONTINUE DOWN THE PATH.

WE'LL SURPRISE 'EM ONE WAY OR THE OTHER!

YES, SIR! LET'S GO MEN...

Teddy had a bunch of newspaper reporters with him, including *Stephen Crane*, famous for writing the Civil War novel *The Red Badge of Courage*.

I DON'T SEE ANYTHING....

LOOK — THIS BARBED-WIRE FENCE HAS BEEN CUT!

RECENTLY, TOO — THE ENDS HAVEN'T *RUSTED* YET...

...I KNOW THAT FROM MY RANCHING DAYS!

Bullets suddenly rained down on them through the leaves, "*making a sound like the ripping of a silk dress.*"

THEY SEE US! SCATTER!

RRRIPPP!

RRIIPPP!

It was Teddy's first taste of real battle, and it was *terrifying.*

"I had an *awful* time trying to get into the fight and trying to do what was right when in it..."

"...and all the while I was thinking that I was the *only* man who did not know what I was about, and that all the *others* did..."

"...whereas, as I found out later, pretty much everybody *else* was as much in the dark as *I* was."

COLONEL! UP THERE! SEE?

YES, I SEE, I SEE!

Teddy wrote, "I was wearing my sword, which in thick jungle now and then got between my legs —"

LET'S GO GET 'EM — **ERK!**

"— from that day on it always went corded in the baggage."

THWOP!

The Americans drove the Spanish back with withering fire, then a charge from both columns sent the enemy running.

YEEE-HAW! "LOOK AT THOSE YANKEES RUN!"

The Americans marched toward the second largest city in Cuba, *Santiago.*

High hills, guarded by over 5000 Spanish troops, protected Santiago from the jungle beyond.

Kettle Hill

San Juan Hill

Santiago

The Signal Corps surveyed the area in a hot-air balloon that made good target practice for the Spanish.

On July 1, 1898, the Rough Riders attacked Kettle Hill with the all-African-American 10th Cavalry, famously dubbed *"Buffalo Soldiers"* by Native Americans either because of their fierce fighting in the Indian Wars...

...or for their *curly hair*, like a buffalo's...

...or *both!*

Teddy would famously call this *"my crowded hour."*

Gatling guns, one of the earliest machine guns, helped their advance by pinning down the enemy at the top of Kettle Hill.

POW POW POW POW POW POW

Spanish fire broke up the regiments and black and white troops quickly became mixed together.

"ARE YOU AFRAID TO STAND UP WHEN I AM ON HORSEBACK?"

Teddy rode his horse to better direct his men, but that made him an easier target for the Spanish troops.

As they charged up the hill, a Spaniard leaped forward to attack Teddy, but he shot the man dead with his revolver –

KRAK

– a revolver that had been recovered from the wreck of the *Maine*.

64

There was heavy hand-to-hand fighting at the top, but a Buffalo Soldier planted the American Flag once the Spaniards were beaten back.

At the same time, another American force had attacked nearby San Juan Heights.

Teddy saw that the enemy had the Americans pinned down and decided to help by leading his troops from Kettle Hill across a ravine to San Juan.

the 24th & 25th Infantry, two more African-American units

LET'S GO MEN — **CHARGE!**

?!

WHA—?

At first, only five men followed him because they couldn't *hear* him.

I SAID, "CHARGE"!!

OH, I THOUGHT YOU SAID, "MARGE."

WHICH WOULD HAVE BEEN WEIRD.

Future World War I hero Lt. Gen. *"Black Jack"** Pershing, present at the battle, remembered:

"White regiments, black regiments, regulars and Rough Riders, representing the young manhood of the North and South, fought shoulder to shoulder, unmindful of race or color, unmindful of whether commanded by an ex-Confederate or not, and mindful of only their common duty as Americans."

Even though the *charge up San Juan Hill* made Teddy an instant *hero* and media star back home...

* He got the nickname for commanding the all-African-American Buffalo Soldiers.

...the fighting was actually *over* by the time they started to the top!

WE'RE... UH...HERE TO *RESCUE* YOU?

WE'RE GOOD! THANKS!

To add insult to injury, Teddy got yelled at by his commanding officer for abandoning Kettle Hill instead of staying to turn back a counterattack.

But soon the Americans were *victorious* – in both the battle *and* the war.

OUR TEDDY FOR OUR GOVERNOR

Now adding *"war hero"* to his list of other accomplishments, Teddy was surprised to learn that the Republicans had nominated him to become governor of his home state of New York.

Teddy campaigned throughout the state, often with fellow Rough Riders. One of his enthusiastic veterans said, meaning to be *helpful:*

"WHEN IT CAME TO THE GREAT DAY HE LED US UP SAN JUAN HILL LIKE *SHEEP TO THE SLAUGHTER* AND SO WILL HE LEAD YOU."

STOP "HELPING," PLEASE.

TEDDY

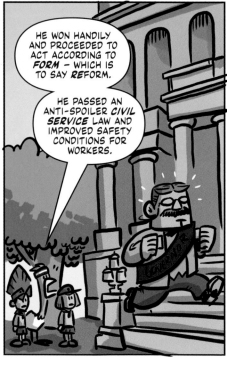

HE WON HANDILY AND PROCEEDED TO ACT ACCORDING TO *FORM* — WHICH IS TO SAY *REFORM.*

HE PASSED AN ANTI-SPOILER *CIVIL SERVICE* LAW AND IMPROVED SAFETY CONDITIONS FOR WORKERS.

This made him very popular to the *voters* and made the elites in government and business very *nervous.*

THIS ROOSEVELT HAS BEEN A *PAIN IN OUR BUTTS* EVER SINCE HE FIRST TOOK PUBLIC OFFICE!

BUT PEOPLE *LOVE* HIM! WE CAN'T JUST *DUMP* HIM! OUR VOTERS WILL TURN ON US!

THERE MUST BE *SOMEWHERE* WE CAN STICK HIM WHERE HE CAN'T DO ANY *DAMAGE....*

WAIT... *I* KNOW...

ARE *YOU* THINKING WHAT *I'M* THINKING?

YES...

VICE PRESIDENT

...LET'S MAKE HIM *VICE PRESIDENT!*

THE AMERICAN

...comes out of the US's weird method of national elections popularly known as the *Electoral College.*

The Constitution *first* said that electors could vote for *two* people for president, so long as one vote was *not* for someone from the same state *as* that elector.

DUDE! I CAN'T VOTE FOR WASHY-G TWICE, DUDE?

NO WAY, DUDE! YOU'RE FROM VIRGINIA TOO! VOTE FOR J-ADAMS FROM MASSACHUSETTS, THOUGH. HE'S A RIGHTEOUS DUDE, DUDE!

The person who got the *most* votes became president, and the person who got the *second* most votes became *vice* president.

Though the Constitution was originally designed *not* to work with a *two-party* system, a two-party system developed immediately after the administration of the first president, George Washington.

The problems with *vice-president-as-second-place* under this system quickly became obvious, in that it forced two political *enemies* to work together in the same government.

Sounds like a nice and noble idea in *theory,* but the reality was kind of a *nightmare.*

VICE PRESIDENT...

So in 1804 the *Twelfth Amendment* to the Constitution was passed, which made electors vote for president and vice president *separately.*

Political parties run *both* candidates on a single *"ticket."*

The Constitution only gives the VP a *couple* of powers, the most important of which, of course, is his *"understudy"* role, becoming president in the event of his boss's death or removal.

IT'S *MY* TIME TO SHINE!

John Adams, Vice Prez #1 (1789-1797)

He's also the president of the Senate, meaning he casts the *tie-breaking vote* when needed...

...but while he's supposed to be *present* for debates, he's not actually allowed to *say* anything.

All of this was so frustrating to the nation's first vice president, John Adams, that he declared the vice presidency was:

"THE MOST *INSIGNIFICANT* OFFICE THAT EVER THE INVENTION OF MAN CONTRIVED OR HIS IMAGINATION *CONCEIVED!"*

President McKinley's first vice president, New Jersey senator **Garret Hobart**, died of heart disease on November 21, 1899.

Republican leaders asked Governor Roosevelt if he would join their **"ticket"** as the new vice-presidential nominee.

Teddy knew his enemies in New York State wanted to get rid of him, but he wanted to stay.

VP

SNEAK! SNEAK!

He knew that vice presidents **rarely** became president **themselves**; it was an obscure position where political dreams **ended.**

Still, Teddy was so popular around the country that he couldn't stop Republican delegates from nominating him on their own.

⇥SIGH⇤

#2

#2

He soon found himself in the middle of the **Election of 1900**, campaigning around the country for McKinley, again with fellow **Rough Riders.**

HOW **DARE** YOU WRITE LYIN' ARTICLES ABOUT **MAH COLONEL** IN YOUR NEWSPAPER?!

PLEASE STOP "HELPING."

Roosevelt's popularity helped win a landslide Electoral College victory for the Republican ticket, 292 to 155.

Teddy's enemies in Washington thought the Republicans were making a big mistake.

"DON'T ANY OF YOU REALIZE THAT THERE'S ONLY *ONE LIFE* BETWEEN THIS *MADMAN* AND THE PRESIDENCY?"

Senator Mark Hanna (1837-1904), R-Ohio

Six months after the inauguration, President McKinley went to *Buffalo, New York*, to attend the Pan-American Exposition, a *World's Fair* celebrating the New World's accomplishments.

WORLD BALANCE

THE NEWSPAPERS REPORTED THAT MCKINLEY WOULD GREET THE PUBLIC ON THE AFTERNOON OF SEPTEMBER 6 AT THE *TEMPLE OF MUSIC*, A CONCERT HALL ON THE FAIRGROUNDS.

A receiving line formed of people coming to greet the president and shake his hand.

One of the people in line was **Leon Czolgosz,** a troubled man who had failed at everything he had ever tried.

He had a vague interest in **anarchism** – the belief that humanity would be better off if **all** governments were **gotten rid of.**

HELLO. THANK YOU FOR COMING, YOUNG MAN.

HOW DO YOU –

KRAK

KRAK

WHAT...?!

UGH!

Before Czolgosz could shoot a *third* time, the man behind him in line, a tall African American from Atlanta named James Parker, *punched* him in the neck!

OOF!

WOK!

"GET THE GUN! GET THE GUN!"

"I HAVE DONE MY DUTY!"

"DON'T LET THEM HURT HIM."

"DON'T LET HIM GET AWAY!"

"HANG HIM – GET THE ROPE!"

But his rescuers were too late – President McKinley had been mortally wounded, and died eight days later.

On September 13, an Adirondacks park guide ran toward a vacationing Teddy bearing a telegram that said McKinley was dying.

Teddy was asked to come to Buffalo. He raced there as soon as he could, arriving not long after the president had passed.

On September 14, in the Buffalo home of Teddy's friend Ashley Wilcox...

"I SHALL TAKE THE OATH AT ONCE."

"AND IN THIS HOUR OF DEEP AND TERRIBLE NATIONAL BEREAVEMENT I WISH TO STATE THAT IT SHALL BE MY AIM...

"...TO CONTINUE ABSOLUTELY *UNBROKEN* THE POLICY OF PRESIDENT MCKINLEY FOR THE PEACE, PROSPERITY, AND THE HONOR OF OUR BELOVED COUNTRY."

"PLEASE RAISE YOUR RIGHT HAND AND REPEAT AFTER ME:

"I, THEODORE ROOSEVELT..."

"I, THEODORE ROOSEVELT..."

At the same time, almost 400 miles away in Manhattan, an unemployed bartender named *John F. Schrank* had a strange dream.

ZZZz

PRESIDENT MCKINLEY?!

"THIS IS MY MURDERER! AVENGE MY DEATH!"

THE — THE VICE PRESIDENT? *HE* HAD YOU KILLED?!

Schrank would think about that dream a lot over the next eleven years, until finally he decided to act on it.

CAN IT... CAN IT BE POSSIBLE?

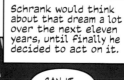

Meanwhile, Teddy instantly *inherited* all the unfinished work of the McKinley Administration...

SOMETHING'S BLOCKING THE DOOR!

...not the least of which was the White House's attempt to get a *canal* built between the Atlantic and Pacific Oceans through the *Isthmus ("narrow strip of land")* *of Panama* in what was then *Colombia.*

PANAMA

Teddy wrote, "During the nearly *four hundred years* that had elapsed since Balboa crossed the Isthmus, there had been a good deal of talk about building an Isthmus canal."

Vasco Núñez de Balboa (1475-1519), 1st European to reach the Pacific from the Atlantic

ATLANTIC

SO *CLOSE* AND YET *SO FAR!*

PACIFIC

SHORTCUT

SOUTH AMERICA

Such a canal would greatly reduce the time and dangers of shipping, as in order to go from one ocean to the other, vessels had to dare the hazardous Cape Horn, south of Argentina.

The United States, partly out of a *Monroe Doctrine*-type attempt to keep the Europeans out of the Western hemisphere...

I'LL TAKE CARE OF THIS!

...agreed to pay for, build, and *maintain* the canal for the good of the *whole world* (and of course the US).

But Colombia wanted more *money* for the land, so it rejected the original canal treaty.

There was already an *independence movement* within the State of Panama, which the Roosevelt administration now felt free to support.

PANAMA

COLOMBIA

HELP!

$?

Panamanians rose up on November 3, 1903, and seized Colombian officials and army officers, imprisoning them without bloodshed.

An American gunboat showed up and landed sailors and marines *"to protect American interests,"* but mostly to discourage a Colombian counterattack. Panama declared its *independence*.

Critics accused the United States of masterminding the whole thing.

YOU *STOLE* PANAMA FROM US! HOW DARE YOU?!

José Manuel Marroquín, Prez #4 (of Colombia – 1900-1904)

WHAT EVER DO YOU MEAN?

WE WANTED OUR CANAL – PANAMA WANTED THEIR COUNTRY!

IT WAS A COMPLETELY FAIR TRADE!

OUR FORCES DIDN'T FIRE A SHOT – THANKS TO YOU! IT WAS SMART YOU DIDN'T START ANY MORE...

...VIOLENCE.

GULP!

People called Teddy's foreign policy "Big Stick Diplomacy."

TALK SOFTLY – BUT ALWAYS CARRY A BIG ARMY!

He talked peacefully – more peacefully than many people thought possible – but the threat of America's military always hung in the air!

Soon the Panama Canal Treaty was signed by the new nation and the USA, which gave the United States power over the Canal Zone itself, and construction on the waterway began.

Wielding this stick, Teddy helped negotiate the end of a **strike** between coal miners and mine owners that could have led to many families **freezing** in the winter of 1902...

....he helped to negotiate an end to a war between Russia and Japan in 1905, which made him the first US president to win the **Nobel Peace Prize**...

...and he forced Britain, Germany, and Italy to back down from their blockade of **Venezuela** over that country's failure to pay their foreign debt!

BOO

VENEZUELA

The US took charge in Europe's dealings with Latin and South America in what became known as the **"Roosevelt Corollary"** to the Monroe Doctrine.

Teddy brought his big stick to *domestic* policy too, breaking up companies that were unfairly shutting out their smaller competitors.

"A *democracy* can be such in *fact* only if there is some rough approximation in similarity in *stature* among the men composing it.

"ONE OF US CAN DEAL IN OUR PRIVATE LIVES WITH THE GROCER OR THE BUTCHER OR THE CHICKEN RAISER, OR IF WE *ARE* THE GROCER OR CARPENTER OR BUTCHER OR FARMER WE CAN DEAL WITH OUR *CUSTOMERS* BECAUSE WE ARE ALL ABOUT THE *SAME SIZE*."

BUT "THERE HAD BEEN IN OUR COUNTRY A RIOT OF INDIVIDUALISTIC MATERIALISM, UNDER WHICH COMPLETE FREEDOM FOR THE *INDIVIDUAL*...

"...TURNED OUT IN PRACTICE TO MEAN PERFECT FREEDOM FOR THE *STRONG* TO RULE THE *WEAK*."

"I was opposed by both the foolish *radicals* who desired to break up *all* big business..."

DOWN

NO $$$

BOO

TEAR IT ALL DOWN!

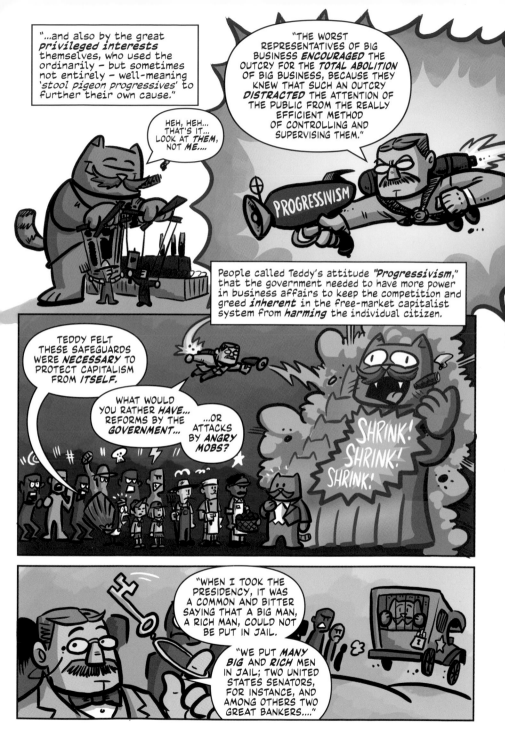

"...and also by the great *privileged interests* themselves, who used the ordinarily – but sometimes not entirely – well-meaning 'stool pigeon progressives' to further their own cause."

"THE WORST REPRESENTATIVES OF BIG BUSINESS *ENCOURAGED* THE OUTCRY FOR THE *TOTAL ABOLITION* OF BIG BUSINESS, BECAUSE THEY KNEW THAT SUCH AN OUTCRY *DISTRACTED* THE ATTENTION OF THE PUBLIC FROM THE REALLY EFFICIENT METHOD OF CONTROLLING AND SUPERVISING THEM."

HEH, HEH... THAT'S IT... LOOK AT *THEM*, NOT *ME*....

PROGRESSIVISM

People called Teddy's attitude *"Progressivism,"* that the government needed to have more power in business affairs to keep the competition and greed *inherent* in the free-market capitalist system from *harming* the individual citizen.

TEDDY FELT THESE SAFEGUARDS WERE *NECESSARY* TO PROTECT CAPITALISM FROM *ITSELF.*

WHAT WOULD YOU RATHER *HAVE*... REFORMS BY THE *GOVERNMENT*...

...OR ATTACKS BY *ANGRY MOBS?*

SHRINK! SHRINK! SHRINK!

"WHEN I TOOK THE PRESIDENCY, IT WAS A COMMON AND BITTER SAYING THAT A BIG MAN, A RICH MAN, COULD NOT BE PUT IN JAIL.

"WE PUT *MANY BIG* AND *RICH* MEN IN JAIL; TWO UNITED STATES SENATORS, FOR INSTANCE, AND AMONG OTHERS TWO GREAT BANKERS...."

THE SQUARE DEAL...

After Upton Sinclair's novel *The Jungle* was published, exposing the **disgusting practices** of the meat industry...

WOULD YOU LIKE ME TO **SUPERSIZE** THAT?

...Teddy created a federal agency, the **Food and Drug Administration**, to inspect what we put in our bodies to make sure it was safe.

Teddy protected **230 million acres** of public land from private exploitation and **doubled** the size of our National Park System.

"KEEP THIS GREAT **WONDER** OF NATURE AS IT NOW IS! LEAVE IT AS IT IS, YOU **CAN NOT IMPROVE** ON IT."

...was what Teddy called his many, many domestic programs that protected the weak from the **thoughtlessness** of the powerful.

IT'S **TYRANNY!!** HE'S A **KING!!**

WHO'S **THAT** GUY?

OH, HE SHOWS UP TO SAY THE SAME THING IN EVERY BOOK.

Certainly, Teddy did things the Founding Fathers
never thought a president should do.

Previous presidents avoided doing things other than what the Constitution said they could do.

LET'S SEE....AM I **ALLOWED** TO END SLAVERY ON MY OWN...? DOESN'T **LOOK** LIKE IT....

We The People

~TEE HEE!~ THAT TICKLES!

Prez #16 (1861-1865)

For the first 125 years of America's existence, **Congress** was thought of as the **main** branch of government, as it had the power to **make** laws.

I'LL HANDLE THIS, PREZ-BOY!

HOLY **SEPARATION OF POWERS,** CONGRESS-MAN!

But Teddy began many of his programs by **Executive Order,** bypassing Congress completely.

DOES THE CONSTITUTION SAY WE **SHOULDN'T** DO IT?

We The People

NOT...NOT REALLY...

THEN LET'S GO FOR IT!

This expansion of powers made people see the presidents after him **differently** – as the main, most **important** person in government.

LEMME AT 'EM, PREZ-MAN!

HOLD ON, **CONGRESS KID!** IT MAY BE...**TOO DANGEROUS!**

NOW, PRESIDENT ROOSEVELT *HATED* BEING CALLED *"TEDDY"*...

SORRY, TEDDY.

GRRRR...

PAT! PAT!

USA

...but one incident *early* in his presidency cemented the nickname forever.

He kept going on hunting trips even while in the White House, and one took him to Mississippi to stalk black bear.

He and his guides looked and looked but couldn't find any...

...so he went back to camp...

...but his guides weren't going to disappoint the most powerful and famous person in the country!

They located a rather small black bear on their own...

...and knocked him out with a rifle butt!

They went and found Teddy, and asked him if he wanted to shoot the bear.

Teddy refused, saying it was bad sport to kill a helpless animal.

WHAT A POOR CREATURE!

The story became public, and cartoonist *Clifford K. Berryman* drew a picture of the incident that made the bear into a cute little cub.

An enterprising Brooklyn toy maker named *Morris Michtom* saw the cartoon and decided to make a doll of the bear itself.

He put the bear in the window of his shop and it became an instant bestseller!

He sent one to the White House, and the president gave Michton permission to call them *"Teddy Bears"* – the same name they have today!

WOW, WHAT A GREAT STORY!

AND THAT FREED BEAR LIVED HAPPILY EVER AFTER?

OH, NO. TEDDY JUST WOULDN'T *SHOOT* IT.

THE GUIDES CUT ITS THROAT!

GGAAHAAHH

I'M GOING TO *CHARGE* YOU NOW FOR THE *THERAPY* I'LL NEED AS AN *ADULT!!*

TOUGH, BUT FAIR.

$

A teddy bear or three likely found their way into the hands of Teddy and Edith's kids. Son *Quentin* Roosevelt and his friends formed what became known as...

THE WHITE HOUSE GANG

Edward "Slates" Stead (the skinny one)

Charlie *"Taffy"* Taft (the big one)

Quentin R.

Rosewell Pickney (son of a White House steward)

Walker White (the small one)

But the most active member was Teddy *himself*. As people liked to note:

"YOU MUST ALWAYS REMEMBER THAT THE PRESIDENT IS ABOUT *SIX*."

They got into all sorts of trouble around 1600 Pennsylvania Avenue.

TAKE *THAT*, BLOODY, BLOODY ANDREW JACKSON!

THIS ONE'S FOR THE CHEROKEE!!

PTui.

Ptui!

Quentin's best friend, *"Taffy,"* aka Charlie Taft, was the son of his *father's* best friend, the Secretary of War, *William Howard Taft.*

Taft joined Teddy's cabinet in *1904*, the year the president ran for his own term in office.

Teddy won the biggest popular margin in American history (at that time): 2.5 million votes! (Electoral College: 330 to 136...a landslide).

YEEEHAW!

Though technically Teddy had only been elected president *once*, he would serve nearly *two full terms* – over two-thirds of *McKinley's* term plus one on his own.

And *no* president, following the example set by George Washington, had ever served more than two terms.

So Teddy proclaimed, even before his next term in office started...

I WILL *NOT* RUN FOR PRESIDENT *AGAIN!*

GASP!

His family and friends were shocked. Teddy would leave office as the *youngest* ex-president ever. There was no law against him running for a third term – was he really sure this is what he wanted to do?

At the 1908 Republican Convention delegates waved toy bears.

WE WANT TEDDY! WE WANT TEDDY!

DOUBLE GULP!

Still, Taft was easily elected after Teddy left the White House.

While on safari in Africa, Teddy became increasingly alarmed at news from home saying Taft *turned back* some of Teddy's policies.

THIS IS JUST *NOT* BULLY!

TAFT THINKS FOR SELF

His government was more *pro-business*. Taft turned over many public lands to private hands!

Prez #27 (1909-1913)

Teddy may have been kicking himself that he had left office too soon.

I WILL NOT RUN —

DON'T SAY IT!!

Time Machine (not actually a thing)

He returned to America as a candidate *against* Taft for the Republican nomination for president in the election of 1912!

I'M BAAAAACK!

President Taft was *completely crushed* by Teddy's betrayal. A reporter found the president in his campaign train, weeping:

"ROOSEVELT WAS MY *CLOSEST FRIEND.*"

The pro-Roosevelt forces showed up – full of confidence – for the Republican Convention in Chicago.

But Teddy still had many enemies in the party, and they were sick of what they saw as his anti-business meddling. They renominated President *Taft* instead.

Teddy wasn't about to give up. He decided to run against both the Republican Taft *and* the Democratic nominee, New Jersey governor *Woodrow Wilson*, under a new, *third* party – with a third animal *mascot!*

I FEEL "AS STRONG AS A *BULL MOOSE!*"

THE PROGRESSIVES

Teddy campaigned tirelessly throughout the country, attacking Taft and Wilson both.

On October 14, Teddy was entering an auditorium in Milwaukee, Wisconsin, to give a speech.

In the crowd was John Schrank — remember him?

He was still haunted by the voice of President McKinley demanding vengeance in his dreams.

"THIS IS MY MURDERER! AVENGE MY DEATH!"

He got as close to Teddy as he could.

BANG

The crowd attacked Schrank, wanting to kill him, but Teddy rose to his feet, asking for mercy.

"STAND BACK! DON'T HURT HIM!"

Schrank spent the rest of his life in a mental institution.

Incredibly, Teddy went to the Progressive Party rally...and gave his speech, *as planned!*

"I SHALL ASK YOU TO BE QUIET AS POSSIBLE. I DON'T KNOW WHETHER YOU FULLY UNDERSTAND THAT I HAVE JUST BEEN *SHOT...*"

GASP!

Teddy knew from inflicting enough bullet wounds on other living things that he was not wounded *badly.* He wasn't coughing up *blood,* so the bullet couldn't have entered his *lungs.*

Miraculously, his folded speech and glasses case had *slowed* the bullet!

"...BUT IT TAKES MORE THAN *THAT* TO KILL A *BULL MOOSE!*"

RAAAAHH!

He finished his speech before going to the hospital! It was *dramatic stuff...*

97

...but it didn't *help*.

Third parties have always been a tough sell in American presidential elections.

The Electoral College is a *winner-take-all* system, meaning whoever gets the most votes in each state gets *all* of that state's *electoral* votes.

TOTES CONGRATS, DUDE!

BEAT IT, LOSER!

If, say, states handed out electoral votes based on *percentage* of the total popular vote, that would encourage more than *two* choices, because you'd have *something* to show even for a loss.

But as it is now, to win as many *states* as possible, you need as *big* a party as you can get!

Teddy's third-party run did what third-party runs tend to do: it *split* one side of the voting public – in this case, people who usually vote *Republican*.

BEAT IT, LOSERS!

Teddy and Taft each got fewer votes than the Democrat, *Woodrow Wilson*, who became president.

Prez #28 (1913-1921)

In defeat, Teddy found himself in political exile. His Republican friends shunned him for going against the party.

Then he received an unexpected offer: a museum in *Argentina* invited him to come south to speak.

¡HOLA!

Upon arriving in South America, however, the Brazilian *Foreign minister* suggested an even bigger challenge: exploring his country's *Rio de Duvida*, or *River of Doubt.*

PERHAPS ONCE YOU FIND ITS MYSTERIOUS *BEGINNING*, IT WILL EVEN BE NAMED *AFTER* YOU!

BULLY!

And so Teddy set off on one last great adventure...

...into the *unknown.*

Everyone risked their lives on the dangerous journey.

Accompanying Teddy were his son *Kermit* and famed Brazilian explorer *Cândido Rondon.*

The expedition's canoes had to be carried around dangerous rapids and waterfalls.

They followed telegraph lines cut through the jungle —

— and the graves of the men who had died stringing them!

It rained constantly.

The worst pests, beyond even *jaguars* and *piranhas* and *poison frogs* and *electric fish*, were the insects –

– bloodsucking flies and small stingless bees called *"eye-lickers"* that blinded you by...

...well, *licking your eyes.*

LICK!

LICK!

YAAAHHH!!

You had to check your poncho before going to bed to make sure it wasn't full of bugs.

Termites ate off an entire leg of Teddy's long underwear!

–:SIGH:–

They were nearly sucked in by whirlpools. Their canoes overturned, losing much of their food and supplies.

Kermit was nearly drowned in the disaster, and one of his porters was not so lucky.

They lost their maps and Teddy had to navigate by the stars.

One of their porters murdered another and ran away, stealing a substantial amount of provisions.

He was never heard from again. Most likely, he ran across a tribe of **cannibals**.

Everyone got sick. Kermit got malaria. Teddy slipped and reopened an old leg injury.

The wound became infected, and he began drifting in and out of consciousness, muttering the same lines of poetry over and over.

"Kubla Khan: or, A Vision in a Dream" by Samuel Taylor Coleridge (1797)

"IN XANADU DID KUBLA KHAN, A STATELY PLEASURE-DOME DECREE...

"IN XANADU DID KUBLA KHAN, A STATELY PLEASURE-DOME DECREE...

I DON'T BELIEVE HE CAN LIVE THROUGH THE NIGHT!

Who knows what strange visions he saw in his fever dreams?

COME ON IN, TEEDIE! THE WATER'S GREAT!

DEAD SEAL?! IS THAT YOU?!

DAD, LOOK OUT! THOSE'RE MAN-EATING PIRANHAS!

OHHH... THEY LOOK FRIENDLY...!

The expedition was successful – they found the river's **headwaters**, where it began.

The River of Doubt was officially renamed **"The River of Roosevelt,"** and the Brazilian state containing the head-waters became **Rondonîa**, after his fellow explorer.

WHOOP-DE-DOO!

RIO ROOSEVELT

Finally, they stumbled upon a **rubber farm** where they were rescued by workers.

"BUT IS HE **REALLY** A PRESIDENT?"

After years and years of pushing himself in **every** aspect of life, Teddy had finally pushed himself **too far.**

He returned to New York thin and weak, almost as if he had turned back into the **sickly boy** he had been born as.

Not long after he returned, America entered *World War I* on the side of her allies Britain and France.

BULLY, WOODY – >KOF!< – I'LL GET THE >KOF!< *ROUGH RIDERS* BACK TOGETHER. WE'LL WHIP THE GERMANS – >KOF!< >KOF!!<

AH...THANKS SO MUCH, MR. PRESIDENT, BUT...UH...

I THINK THE TIME FOR ADVENTURE HAS *PASSED* FOR YOU....

OH...I SUPPOSE YOU MAY BE RIGHT...!

IT WAS NICE OF YOU TO LET THE OLD MAN DOWN *EASY* LIKE THAT, MR. PRESIDENT....

ARE YOU NUTS? I DID THAT FOR *ME*!

GIVE THAT GUY AN *INCH* AND HE TAKES A *MILE*!

YOU THINK I WANT TO RUN AGAINST *WORLD WAR I HERO* THEODORE ROOSEVELT IN *1918*?!

Soon Quentin was flying combat missions over Europe.

On July 14, 1918, Quentin and his five-plane unit fought seven *German* planes led by Herman Göring, who would go on to build *Hitler's* air force.

Suddenly, Quentin realized another German squadron was on their trail!

He turned to engage them alone so his squad could get away.

Quentin was shot down and crashed in German territory.

The Germans buried him near the crash site, with a crude cross of saplings lashed together with the wire from his plane.

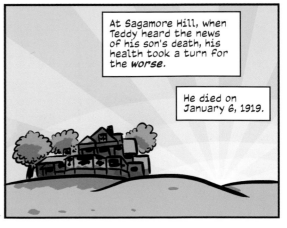

At Sagamore Hill, when Teddy heard the news of his son's death, his health took a turn for the *worse*.

He died on January 6, 1919.

"THE CREDIT BELONGS TO THE MAN WHO IS ACTUALLY *IN* THE ARENA..."

"...WHOSE FACE IS MARRED BY *DUST* AND *SWEAT* AND *BLOOD*; WHO STRIVES VALIANTLY; WHO ERRS AND COMES *SHORT* AGAIN AND AGAIN..."

"...BECAUSE THERE IS NO EFFORT WITHOUT *ERROR* OR *SHORT-COMING*; BUT WHO DOES ACTUALLY STRIVE TO *DO* THE DEEDS; WHO KNOWS THE GREAT *ENTHUSIASMS*..."

FWOOOOSH!

"...SO THAT HIS PLACE SHALL *NEVER* BE WITH THOSE COLD AND TIMID SOULS WHO NEITHER KNOW VICTORY *NOR* DEFEAT."

ROAR

HEY, YOU GUYS! MISS US?

WHEW! THANK GOODNESS! WE WERE LOOKING ALL OVER FOR YOU TWO!

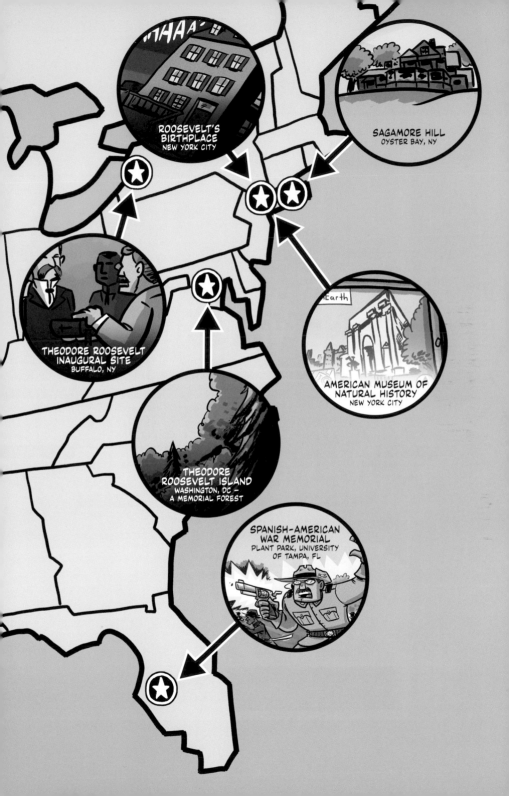

ROOSEVELT'S
BIRTHPLACE
NEW YORK CITY

SAGAMORE HILL
OYSTER BAY, NY

THEODORE ROOSEVELT
INAUGURAL SITE
BUFFALO, NY

Earth

AMERICAN MUSEUM OF
NATURAL HISTORY
NEW YORK CITY

THEODORE
ROOSEVELT ISLAND
WASHINGTON, DC —
A MEMORIAL FOREST

SPANISH–AMERICAN
WAR MEMORIAL
PLANT PARK, UNIVERSITY
OF TAMPA, FL

TIMELINE

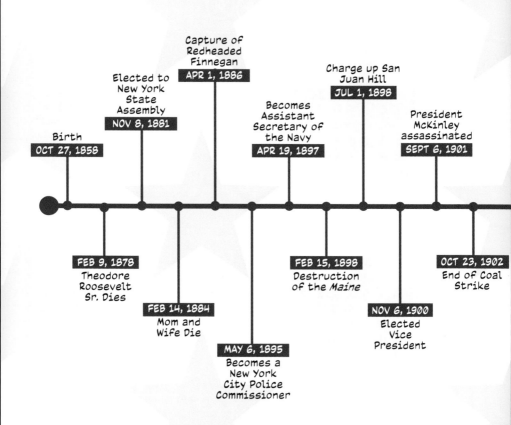

Birth
OCT 27, 1858

Elected to New York State Assembly
NOV 8, 1881

Capture of Redheaded Finnegan
APR 1, 1886

Becomes Assistant Secretary of the Navy
APR 19, 1897

Charge up San Juan Hill
JUL 1, 1898

President McKinley assassinated
SEPT 6, 1901

FEB 9, 1878
Theodore Roosevelt Sr. Dies

FEB 14, 1884
Mom and Wife Die

MAY 6, 1895
Becomes a New York City Police Commissioner

FEB 15, 1898
Destruction of the *Maine*

NOV 6, 1900
Elected Vice President

OCT 23, 1902
End of Coal Strike

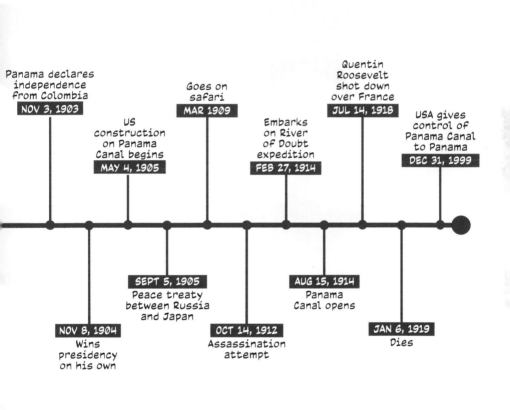

Panama declares
independence
from Colombia
NOV 3, 1903

US
construction
on Panama
Canal begins
MAY 4, 1905

Goes on
safari
MAR 1909

Embarks
on River
of Doubt
expedition
FEB 27, 1914

Quentin
Roosevelt
shot down
over France
JUL 14, 1918

USA gives
control of
Panama Canal
to Panama
DEC 31, 1999

SEPT 5, 1905
Peace treaty
between Russia
and Japan

AUG 15, 1914
Panama
Canal opens

NOV 8, 1904
Wins
presidency
on his own

OCT 14, 1912
Assassination
attempt

JAN 6, 1919
Dies

AMENDMENT (n): a change to the US constitution (there are 27 as of this writing)

ASSAILANT (n): somebody who attacks someone else

BEREAVEMENT (n): the feeling of losing a loved one

CAMOUFLAGE (n): hiding soldiers and their equipment by blending them in with their surroundings

CONTRIVE (v): create a situation on purpose

COROLLARY (n): a direct result of something else

CORRUPTION (n): dishonest acts by people in power, often involving money

DEBATE (n): a formal discussion in which both sides of the same argument are presented

DESOLATE (adj): sad and empty

FLEET (n): a group of ships sailing together

HAZARDOUS (adj): risky, dangerous

INAUGURATION (n): a ceremony to mark the beginning of something (like, say, a presidency)

INSIGNIFICANT (adj): too small to be worth anything

LEGISLATURE (n): the governing body of a country that votes bills into laws

MOMENTUM (n): force gained by the motion of a moving body

OBSCURE (adj): not known about or understood

PROSPERITY (n): being wealthy and/or successful

REGIMENT (n): a large unit of an army, usually commanded by an officer with the rank of colonel

SQUADRON (n): in our book, a group of warships commanded by the same flag officer

TAXIDERMY (n): the art of stuffing and mounting the skin of dead animals so they look like they're still alive

TUMOR (n): an abnormal swelling in the body

THE CONSERVATION PRESIDENT

TEDDY BELIEVED SO STRONGLY IN PROTECTING THE UNITED STATES' WILD LANDS AND CREATURES THAT HE SET ASIDE OVER 230 MILLION ACRES OF LAND FOR THE PUBLIC GOOD:

24 WATER RECLAMATION PROGRAMS

SIX NATIONAL PARKS

51 BIRD SANCTUARIES

18 NATIONAL MONUMENTS

150 NATIONAL FORESTS

4 NATIONAL GAME PRESERVES

BIBLIOGRAPHY

Looker, Earle. *The White House Gang.* New York: Fleming H. Revell Co., 1929. A very rare account of the antics of Quentin Roosevelt's boyhood chums by a member of the "gang," with great illustrations by the legendary artist John Montgomery Flagg.

Millard, Candice. *The River of Doubt: Theodore Roosevelt's Darkest Journey.* New York: Doubleday, 2005. The harrowing story of Teddy's near-fatal expedition into the Amazon.

Miller, Scott. *The President and the Assassin: McKinley, Terror, and Empire at the Dawn of the American Century.* New York: Random House, 2011. The sad story of President William McKinley step-by-step with the life of the man who killed him.

Morris, Edmund. *The Rise of Theodore Roosevelt* and *Theodore Rex.* New York: Modern Library, 1979 and 2001. Morris's two-volume biography of Teddy's youth and presidency remains the definitive take on the subject.

Roosevelt, Theodore. *An Autobiography.* 1913. Teddy wrote a

lot of books, and his life was interesting enough that a lot of those books were about himself. Most of the direct quotes from Teddy in our book come from this one.

Roosevelt, Theodore. *Hunting Trips of a Ranchman* and *The Wilderness Hunter*. New York: Modern Library, 1998. Teddy wrote a lot of books, and his books about nature are among his best. If you love reading about the outdoors, you can't go wrong with him.

Roosevelt, Theodore. *The Rough Riders*. 1899. Did we mention Teddy wrote a lot of books? His adventures in Cuba, in his own words.

Traxel, David. *Crusader Nation: The United States in Peace and the Great War 1898-1920*. New York: Alfred A. Knopf, 2006. A great look at Teddy's world and the effect it had on him – and that he had on it.

Wead, Doug. *All the Presidents' Children: Triumph and Tragedy in the Lives of America's First Families*. New York: Atria Books, 2003. A standard reference here at Action Presidents, with all the adventures of the Roosevelt kids as children and adults.